To: Ha

From: Carl & Janie

" thanks for being
our friends "

And the Moral of the Story Is ...

CARL HART

WESTBOW°
PRESS
A DIVISION OF THOMAS NELSON
& ZONDERVAN

WestBow Press books may be ordered through
booksellers or by contacting:

WestBow Press
A Division of Thomas Nelson & Zondervan
1663 Liberty Drive
Bloomington, IN 47403
www.westbowpress.com
1 (866) 928-1240

ISBN: 978-1-4908-8998-6 (sc)
ISBN: 978-1-4908-9000-5 (e)

Print information available on the last page.

WestBow Press rev. date: 12/02/2015

Contents

Dedication

I dedicate this book to my wife Janie who for forty-eight years has listened to my stories and parables over and over. And yet she continues to encourage and assist me. I say as someone else has said about his wife, Janie "has co-authored my life" and she has been the "wind beneath my wings" of which this book is but a reflection.

Words of Gratitude

I wish to express my gratitude and appreciation to Marcie Brand, my former secretary and longtime friend, for typing the manuscript of this book and for her assistance regarding the layout. Special recognition goes to Strat Burns for her contributions to this project.

Also, my gratitude goes to my two sons, David Carl and Paul Alfred, who have listened to my stories through the years. I am sure it must have been painful at times.

Introduction

At times when I was growing up, my parents would teach us five children with stories and parables. For example, I remember the parable that my dad told many times about the man who borrowed money from the bank, promising to repay it on a certain day. He spent the money foolishly and refused to work so he could repay the bank on the promised date. The moral of Dad's parable was, "Let your word be your bond." That is, don't make a promise you don't intend to keep. Be a person who can be depended upon.

I remember one of the stories my mother would tell about how we should choose our friends. It was about a good boy who was from a good family. He began hanging out with fellows who cussed and drank. One day while he was with them, they broke into a Coke machine and stole the money. The good boy was arrested along with the others because he was with them. Mother's lesson was, to put it in her words, "Birds of a feather flock together." That is, people who have the same ideas and morals run around together. So be careful who you select to be your friends. They may lead you astray.

So through the years I have realized how helpful it can be to seek out the morals and lessons found in stories and parables.

In this book I will attempt to share with the reader some of the stories and parables of my own experiences, attaching a moral lesson to each one.

I trust that the readers of this book might find themselves in some of these stories and be willing to share them with others as well.

Cookies Vs. Parents

Our little four-year-old grandson had been told a number of times that he could not pull a chair up to the kitchen counter and help himself to the cookies in the cookie jar.

One day when little Will's father went out to the street to bring in the garbage can, little Will quickly grabbed a chair and was dragging it toward the kitchen counter when his dad came in the door. The dad said, "Will, what are you doing?" Little Will replied, "Oh, I was not getting cookies!"

And the moral of the story is . . .

You can be sure your parents will find you out.

The Church Bell

Growing up as a boy, we lived close enough to town to hear the church bell ring on Sunday morning at 9:00.

When the church bell rang at 9:00, it was a reminder that it was one hour before Sunday school would start. Then at 10:45 the church bell would ring again, reminding all that Sunday school would dismiss and worship services would begin at 11:00.

The ringing of the church bell was an invitation to come to the church and worship. I can remember as Dad came in the house from outside on Sunday morning he would say, "I just heard the church bell ringing; let's get ready to go."

Mr. Sutton was the bell ringer. However, he would allow us junior age boys to help him at the 10:45 ringing. He tied knots in the bell rope so our hands wouldn't slip. We had to hold on tight so the weight of our bodies could pull the rope down and ring the bell. The weight of the bell would pick us up from the floor and then the weight of our bodies would pull the rope down to ring the bell again. This was fun. And I think Mr. Sutton enjoyed it as much as we did.

One day Mr. Sutton became ill and died. No one took over the task of ringing the bell each Sunday morning. The church bell was never rung again since his death.

I have not heard a church bell ring in years. The church bell called people for hundreds of years to come and worship. Today the church bells are silent.

And the moral of the story is . . .

Could it be that we stopped listening to the church bell and now we listen for the referee's whistle instead?

There Is Some Good in All of Us

While serving as chaplain at the Shelby County Penal Farm in Memphis, Tennessee, I met an inmate who was a painter. He was serving time for "public drunkenness." The five-thousand acre farm was what was called a "work house" where inmates could work out their fines for a public offense if they had no money. He had been in the penal farm many, many times. He would serve ten, twenty or thirty days, get out and then be back the next week. Alcohol had taken its terrible toll, but with a quivering hand he could still paint.

One day he came to my office and told me that he would paint me a picture if I would get him a canvas. After he told me the size he wanted, I asked him about the oils he would need. He informed me that he had plenty of oils and would not need any. Several weeks later when he brought me the painting, I asked him if I could replace the oils that he had used. He replied, "No, no, I always have plenty of oils." Knowing that we didn't have oils in the prison for doing such a painting, I asked, "Where do you get your oils?" He said, "Oh, I get them down at the paint shop. I get those empty paint buckets and dig out the remains in the bottom of the buckets before they get thrown away. It makes good oils for painting"

And the moral of the story is . . .

Maybe this inmate was trying to say something to me with this painting. Maybe he was saying there is still some good in this quivering old hand of an alcoholic and there is some good in all of the other inmates.

Note: This painting now hangs in the prayer chapel of the First Baptist Church of Carrollton, Georgia.

Our Favorite Tree

One morning when I was about twelve years of age, our family was all seated at the table eating breakfast when all of a sudden there was a loud crashing sound outside! We all (five children and Mom and Dad) ran outside to see what had happened. To our shock and surprise, it was our old oak tree. It had split down the middle. Half of it had fallen to the ground and the other half still stood. The tree was hollow inside, and the weight of the huge limbs caused it to split and fall.

It was a very large tree, about thirty-six inches in diameter at the ground. The part that had fallen to the ground had a huge limb on it that held our swing. Dad had made the swing for us. He made the seat wide so two of us could swing at the same time. He also had nailed some steps on the side of the tree, making a ladder so we could climb up in the tree.

The fall of the tree created an awful sight. It was a sad time for us. We had played under the tree almost every day. In hot weather Mom and Dad would take chairs out under the tree where it was cool, and Mom would shell peas or sew. Now our "play tree" had been destroyed. Where would we swing and climb now? I dare say each of us must have shed a tear. Then Dad said, "The old tree served its purpose well."

Dad tried to console us by telling us how old the tree might have been. He said that Civil War soldiers might have slept under the tree because he had found a belt buckle that had belonged to a soldier in the woods just three-hundred yards from our house. It seemed to help matters when he then took us into the house and showed us the belt buckle and let each one of us hold it for a minute or so.

And the moral of the story is . . .

Get over it. Nothing lasts forever except our spirit and God's love.

The Little Church I Wanted to Hug

It was 1951 then and it is 2014 now. The little church had called me as its pastor. It excited me greatly because it was my first church to serve as pastor. I remember driving there that first morning and just sitting there in the parking area for a while being thankful for the opportunity.

I remember the greeting the church gave me and the way the members cared and loved their pastor.

I remember the singing and the special days the church observed with its great food and fellowship.

I recall the big heater that sat in the middle of the floor and how we all gathered around it.

I recall the first funeral I conducted. It was for a little four-year-old girl with beautiful red hair.

I remember how after a time I had to resign and go to another church.

So after sixty years I decided to go back and see the little church building where I first started.

Things had changed, like the parking lot. It was changed to a paved surface and not gravel any more.

The stained glass windows had been removed and plain ones installed.

The tables out back of the church where we once ate our meals on special days were gone.

The little steeple had been removed.

I walked inside, and there were no pews or other furniture. All of it had been replaced with bales of hay and some farm tools.

I sat down on one of the bales of hay. All alone, I just sat there for quite a while. I closed my eyes and remembered the wonderful things and people I had known in that place.

As I walked out and down to my car, I looked back and said to myself, "Old church, you have lost your beautiful windows and your little steeple, but if I could I would put my arms around you and give you a big hug."

And the moral of the story is . . .

Things change, but good memories last forever.

Why Attend Church

Pat, my associate, and myself had a trip that took us to Guam and several other countries in the Far East. Our two-day visit in Guam was great until we got caught in a traffic jam on our way to the airport. We were running so close to missing our flight that Pat hopped out of the car when we arrived at the airport and ran to the gate to check us in.

The clerk expressed his regret and stated that the plane had already left the gate and was awaiting take-off instructions. Pat replied, "We must get on that plane; stop the plane!" The clerk shook his head, "No." Knowing that it would be two days before we could get another flight going to our destination, Pat yelled, "Stop the plane!" This brought out a supervisor to ask how he might help. Pat pulled a paper out of his coat pocket, waved it in the air, and with a loud voice said, "Stop the plane; we are traveling on government orders." The supervisor ran to the phone, stopped the plane and ordered a car to take us out to the runway. We boarded the plane.

After we were in the air, I asked Pat (knowing that I had the government orders in my pocket), "What was that paper you were waving in the air back at the airport?" He pulled the paper from his pocket and handed it to me. It was a church bulletin listing the order of last Sunday's worship service where Pat had attended church.

And the moral of the story is . . .

Go to church and you'll have something to show for it.

I Know an Angel

Through the years I have been asked if I believe in angels. My answer has always been, "Yes, I believe in live ones." I have never seen one with wings like those the artists paint. But I have seen one with DeLange Syndrome. He was an angel all right. As the dictionary says, "A messenger from God." He was born with extreme Down Syndrome. He never spoke a word during his twenty-three years of life. He had to have around-the-clock care. He could remember very little. He paced the floor. He was not a pest; he was a person. God breathed life into him like He did the rest of us. He could smile; he could give you a big hug. But he had no wings.

He didn't need wings or be able to talk. His presence spoke louder than words. His presence asked questions like why him and not me? Why can't he speak when I can? Where was God when this happened? Am I serious about the life God gave me, or am I just playing around? Then the big question: Am I thankful for what I am and who I am? He was an angel all right. I know; I was his grandfather.

And the moral of the story is . . .

There are some questions we can't answer, but some lessons we never forget.

Wrong Sermon Notes

While I was a student in the seminary, I was the speaker in a revival at a church six miles from where I pastored. It was Wednesday night. The pastor and I had rushed to get home from the seminary forty miles away to the home of a church member to have supper and then go on to the church. I had stopped by my house only long enough to freshen up and to pick up my Bible. When I got to the church, I went back to a little room just behind the choir loft where the pastor was waiting for me to pray before going out for the service. We had our prayer and the pastor said, "What subject are you preaching on tonight?" I opened my Bible and looked for my notes only to find out that I had not put the notes in my Bible that I was going to use. I said, "Pastor, I don't have my notes. I have got to go home and get them." He said, "We will keep singing until you get back." So I raised the window, crawled out and took off. (Six miles to my house and the same distance back!)

When I got back to the church, I crawled back through the window and slowly walked out on the speaker's platform and sat down beside the pastor. He said, "I am glad you made it; my wife is on the last hymn that she can play."

I have always felt bad about what happened that night because I might have left the impression that I was back there in that room praying all that time.

And the moral of the story is . . .

Admit your mistakes. Don't try to cover them up. It takes too much covering.

True Friendship

Ten days after I arrived to serve as the chaplain in the Shelby County Penal Farm, Mr. Mark Luttrell came to serve as the warden. We quickly became friends. We needed each other. It was my first position as a chaplain and his first position as a warden. Our friendship grew, and three years later I went to Brushy Mountain State Prison to serve as chaplain. Then I went to Nashville to serve as Director of Chaplaincy for the Tennessee Department of Corrections, and he came to Nashville to serve as Commissioner of Corrections for the State of Tennessee. In 1970 I came to Atlanta to serve at the Home Mission Board. We kept in touch throughout the years. Back in Tennessee we had times when we just talked. Then we had prayer times. All to say, our friendship grew very strong. After I had been in Atlanta several years, he called me from Brushy Mountain State Prison. (Now this was when he was the Commissioner of Corrections for the State of Tennessee.) After we exchanged greetings and family updates, I asked him what he was doing at Brushy Mountain State Prison. He said, "That's why I called you." Then for the next thirty minutes he told me why he was closing the Brushy Mountain State Prison. At the time, the prison had a population of about six hundred. He was closing it because the security guards were on strike after he would not allow them to create a union.

Then he said, "I have been here a week and I have called in the highway patrol for security. I need you to come up and be with me for a couple of days." I went up early the next morning.

He and I talked for a long time. We prayed. Then he told me, "I am closing down the prison tonight. I have buses coming from other institutions, and we are going to ship all the inmates out escorted by the Tennessee Highway Patrol. All the arrangements have been made with the other institutions."

James Earl Ray (assassin of celebrated civil rights leader Martin Luther King Jr.) was at the Brushy Mountain State Prison at the time. Therefore, my next question was, "How will you handle James Earl Ray in all of this?" Mark went to great lengths to tell me the details. Then he said, "Stay with me through the night." The security buses came and took inmates to four different institutions.

It was a long night. The plans worked and the striking guards did not know what was happening until it was done.

When the prison was cleared, we had a cup of coffee and talked for a while. We cherished our friendship and thanked God for His help. Then Mark got in a Tennessee State Patrol car and was off to Nashville.

I never saw him again before he died, but I am reminded of his true friendship from time to time.

And the moral of the story is . . .

Sometimes all we have is a prayer and a friend.

Do You Like Okra?

Dad would "break up" (which means plowing the soil and getting it ready to plant) the garden each spring.

One spring he had my brother Clifford and myself pulling up the old dried okra stalks and burning them. I was at one end of the garden and Clifford was at the other end. We started "chucking" (a word meaning to throw) clods of dirt at each other. One of us chucked a clod of dirt that hit the mule that was pulling Dad's plow. The mule was frightened and ran through the garden fence, plow and all. Dad had told us twice to stop chucking. So without saying a word, he grabbed an okra stalk and whipped both of us. I haven't liked okra since.

And the moral of the story is . . .

Too much play and too little work will lead to regrets.

Smart Dog

This is one of Dad's stories. (He would embellish his stories at times.)

Dad loved to train bird dogs to hunt quail. He would brag on how smart they were. This story is about "Joe," one of Dad's smartest dogs.

Dad told about the day he and Joe were hunting down near the creek. As they approached the creek that was lined with heavy underbrush, Joe pointed. His tail went straight and his body looked as if it was frozen. Dad walked up and kicked in the underbrush. One quail flew up and Dad shot it. Now, Joe didn't move, not one hair. Dad knew that meant there was another quail in the underbrush so he kicked again. Another quail flew up and Dad shot it. Joe didn't move, still frozen in his tracks. Dad kicked again. Another quail flew up and Dad shot it. Still, Joe would not break his point. You see, only when there was no more quail would a good dog break his point and retrieve the shot birds. After three birds, one after the other flying up, Joe still pointed, meaning there was still a quail in the underbrush. Dad kicked again and another quail flew up. Dad did this nine times before Joe broke his point and retrieved nine quail. Dad walked up to where Joe had pointed and discovered that the nine quail had been in a hole to keep warm, and Joe had his paw over the hole to let the quail out one at a time.

And the moral of the story is . . .

Don't believe everything a bird hunter tells you. They are first cousins to fishermen.

Silent Discipline

When I was sixteen I worked at a dairy. My job was to milk fifteen cows by hand each morning and evening. No electric milkers. It was a man's job. Getting up at 4:00 in the morning. Scraping ice off the backs of the cows with a hoe. Cleaning out the barn each morning. But I was paid big bucks, $4.50 a week!

Being the manly person that I was, I thought one Saturday it was time for me to smoke a cigar. So I purchased me a King Edward Cigar and pondered where I could light this thing. Well, a man with a cigar ought to go to the poolroom where the smoke is so thick you can almost cut it with a knife. Now the poolroom was a "joint," a place where men (only) were seen, a place where you could buy beer and learn new cuss words. It was a place Mother and Dad told us never to go. Well, a man with a regular job making $4.50 a week with a cigar in his pocket ought to be able to go there long enough to smoke a cigar. So I did.

My dad was in town and someone told him they saw me go in the poolroom. Well, I had been in there for a while and had taken several good puffs when I looked up and saw dad standing in the doorway. I was lucky I didn't have the cigar in my mouth. When I saw him, I dropped my cigar on the floor. He looked straight at me and motioned for me to come. I went to the door. Dad had it open for me. I went out and got in the truck with him. I sat there wondering what he was going to say or do to me. We rode all the way home with me thinking that. Dead silence all the way. My dad never mentioned the situation to me.

But that was the worst "whipping" I ever got. His silence made an impression on me that I have never forgotten.

And the moral of the story is . . .

There is a time to speak and a time to be silent, meaning at times silence can be more effective than what we have to say.

God Screens
Our Prayers

My oldest brother Clifford and I would go down to the river to fish quite often. We would take food with us because we would stay all day.

One day as we were getting things together to go fishing, Clifford said, "What do we have to eat?" I replied that I had gotten some leftover biscuits and two baked sweet potatoes. As we were leaving Clifford said, "How about that bantam (small species) rooster in the coop?" Our neighbor down the road had bantam chickens and from time to time several of them would wander up to our house. My mother would catch them and put them in the chicken coop. Later she would see our neighbor and tell her one of the bantams had wandered off and was held in our chicken coop. Then the neighbor would come by and get it.

On this day when we were going fishing there was a bantam rooster in the chicken coop. I ran to get a sack, Clifford put that rooster in the sack, and off to the river we ran.

Clifford said, "You pull the feathers off that rooster and I will build a fire so we can roast this bird." Well, it took me a while to do that. Feathers were hard to pull out. Finally after washing it in the river and cleaning out the insides with my hunting knife, I had it ready. As it cooked it seemed to get smaller. Finally it was roasted and ready to eat. Clifford cut off a drumstick with his hunting knife and started to take a bite when I stopped him and said, "We have to say thanks for the food." Clifford said, "You can't thank God for something you stole."

And the moral of the story is . . .

God screens our prayers, and only you know why He does.

Bantam Rooster

Our neighbor came to see Mama and to get her bantam rooster. Mother had to tell her that several days before she had gone to feed the rooster in the coop and it was not there! Mother told her it was a mystery. It just vanished. For days and days Mother would say to us, "What could have happened to that rooster?"

Twenty-seven years later our family got together for a Christmas dinner. When we had finished and were talking about the past, I whispered to Clifford, "This might be a good time to tell Mama what happened to the rooster." So we did.

And the moral of the story is . . .

Waiting until the time is right is very important. Wait until the light is green. Don't go on red. It may take twenty-seven years for the light to change. It is safer to wait.

Hugging Is Needed

Back in the day when our youngest son Paul first started playing Little League, the church had a special awards night for the various teams. Paul received an award! When we got home after the event, we began looking for a place for the award. Finding a place on a shelf in Paul's room, we (his mother, Paul and I) then sat on the side of his bed and talked about the accomplishment he had made and encouraged him regarding the future.

The next night Paul did not want to go to bed; he wanted to stay up a little longer. Finally, after much encouragement, he went up and was soon back down. With further encouragement, he went up again. Later when Janie went up to check on him, as she always did, there was a note on his pillow. Now a note on his pillow was not something new. Several times he had gone to bed and thought of something he was to do the next day regarding school. He would write his mother a note, "I need two dollars to take to school tomorrow," "Please iron my blue shirt," etc.

When Janie went up to check on him that night she found a note on his pillow that read, "Have you hugged your athlete today?"

And the moral of the story is . . .

If our children have to ask for a hug, we are not doing a very good job.

Freedom

When I was a boy of about seven or eight, the convicts (as they were called then) from the Shelby County Penal Farm would come down our gravel road and clean out the gravel that had washed into the ditches and throw it back on the road. (No large equipment in those days to do the job.)

My parents would allow me to go over in the field and watch them. I would get close enough to also hear them. Some were singing, some were talking and laughing as they worked. Once in awhile I would hear cussing. But there was another constant noise. It was the dragging of chains on the gravel road. All the inmates had steel clamps around their ankles and a short length of chain attached to each clamp to prohibit their escaping.

I would watch in the evening when they were preparing to go back to the prison. They put all their tools in the truck which was a bus-like vehicle with bars on the windows. Then the guards would line up all the inmates and cut the chains from their ankles, allowing them to step onto the truck/bus and return to the prison where they were placed behind bars.

And the moral of the story is. . .

Freedom is a precious thing when you have it, but life becomes a yoke of misery when you lose it.

The Race

A creek ran through the little farm that Dad rented when I was growing up as a boy. Mama and Dad would let me play in the creek bed when Dad was plowing on either side of the creek.

The creek was filled with "goodies" such as little green frogs, mounds of sand, birds, and small areas of water to wade in. Now and then a snake would seek attention.

I was not alone. "Too Many," the nickname of my black friend, was always with me. He was given the nickname "Too Many" because he had six toes on each foot. I remember the day his mother Roxie bought him a new pair of shoes and had to cut holes in each shoe because they were not wide enough for his extra toes. Of course, who needed shoes in the summer? The only time we wore shoes in the summer was to attend church.

I must have been about eight years old when one day my dad came in from the field and asked my mother where I was. Mama said, "I called him several times, but he didn't answer." Dad started looking for me and finally spotted "Too Many" and me down at the creek. He went down and hid under the bridge that crossed the creek. As "Too Many" and I were about midway on the bridge, my dad let out a scream that sounded like a bobcat. "Too Many" and I screamed out and took off running for the house, screaming all the way. When we got to the house, Mama had heard us and was out in the yard. When we reached her, both of us were running and crying. She bent over and reached out both arms. "Too Many" fell into one arm and I fell into the other. We were so frightened neither of us could talk. After we had quieted down, Dad walked up. Mama asked him, "What on earth happened?" Dad told her, and they had a few things to say to each other. Finally Dad promised he would not frighten us again.

Years passed, and "Too Many" and I were grown when we met on the street one day. As we talked about growing up, "Too Many" said, "Do you remember the time your dad got under the bridge and frightened us and we ran so fast to the house?" I said, "Yes, I sure do." He replied, "You outran me that day in spite of the fact that I had more traction!"

And the moral of the story is . . .

The rat race of life requires that we give it our best regardless.

My Bicycle

In the 1940s men did not ride bicycles in West Tennessee. It was considered "sissy" or "not manly like," but that didn't stop my dad. It was 1942 when my older brother Clifford joined the Navy. He had a bicycle that he gave me the morning he left.

Now I had saved my money and bought a bicycle for two dollars. It was a pile of junk, no fenders, no chain guard, and no kickstand.

So Clifford's giving me his bicycle was a real "step-up" for me. It was loaded with a carrier on the back and even a light on the front fender. Clifford even gave me a key to the lock that he used with a small length of chain to lock the bicycle so no one else could ride it.

The "Big War" in the 40s brought on the rationing of gasoline. Dad had an old 1929 Chevrolet Roadster that had its canvas top destroyed by a hail storm.

So he had made a pickup truck out of it. It was an eye opener! Mother refused to ride in it any more after the door on her side fell off right in the middle of town.

By this time Dad had stopped farming and was doing carpenter work. He seemed to have enough gas coupons to keep the old truck going until one day my brother-in-law got a job at the airplane factory in Memphis, Tennessee, which was about twenty-five miles away. After about the second week he realized that fifty miles round trip per day would take more rationing stamps than he had. So he started asking Dad for any extra rationing stamps he could spare.

After about two months, Dad sat down with me and explained the situation. He told me, "There is a war going on and each one of us has to do our part to win the war." Then he said, "I am going to park my old truck here in the yard, and I am going back and forth to my work on the bicycle that Clifford gave you. That way I can give all of my gas coupons to your brother-in-law. We will be doing our part to win the war and bring Clifford home."

I nodded my head without saying a word, knowing that he was right. After just sitting there in silence for quite a while, I spoke up and said, "It's ready to go. I just oiled the chain."

So the next morning I watched Dad go out of the driveway on my bicycle while I felt a little mixed up inside.

The next spring Dad took a job restoring an old log cabin, building a barn, and making several gates. The job was located seven miles from our home, fourteen miles round trip. I must admit that I did wonder, war or no war, what those daily trips would do to my bicycle.

Dad treated my bicycle with upmost care, putting it on the back porch at night out of the weather and keeping it serviced, including a new set of tires.

Finally the day came when school was out for the summer. I was fifteen and wondering what I was going to do all summer without my bicycle. That night at the supper table, Dad told me he needed someone to help him paint a barn and some gates, and he wondered if I was interested. He then said the pay would be twenty-five cents an hour. I replied, "That's two dollars a day. I'll take the job!"

The next morning I looked out to see Dad tightening the carrier on the back of the bicycle where I would ride. After breakfast just as it was good daylight, Mother handed me a bucket that contained our lunch. I walked out to my bicycle where Dad was waiting. I threw my leg over the carrier and we were on our way. Seven miles seemed a long way that first morning.

The summer went by fast. I had given up my bicycle, Dad had given up his truck, my brother-in-law worked at a defense plant, the war was won, and Clifford came home.

And the moral of the story is . . .

God didn't waste His creative life on anyone. We all have a place and task under the sun.

What's Right and What's Wrong

My wife Janie and I had finished our meal at the restaurant, and the waitress brought us our check. As she handed it to me, she asked how long my wife and I had been married. Then I asked her how long she had been married. She told us and proceeded to tell us about the wedding and honeymoon. In the process of many details, she told us that she and her husband had bought their wedding outfits at Walmart. After the wedding they took their outfits back to Walmart and got their money back to use to go on their honeymoon.

And the moral of the story is . . .

Dishonesty comes in many forms.

Where Is Truth?

(This is one of Dad's stories.)

Dad and one of his cousins went down to fish at the Wolf River which was about a mile from where we lived. They agreed that one would fish upstream and the other downstream. This separated them, and they couldn't find each other when it was time to go home. So Dad went on home. Some thirty minutes later his cousin walked up. He asked Dad what he caught, and Dad said, "I caught a fifteen-pound fish." Then Dad asked his cousin what he caught. The cousin said that he didn't catch a fish, but he caught his line on something that he pulled up and out of the water. It was an old lantern with the date of 1865 on the bottom. That was the year Abraham Lincoln was assassinated. Dad said, "That is an old lantern." His cousin replied, "And the lantern was still lit, still burning!" My dad then replied, "I'll knock ten pounds off my fish if you will blow out your lantern!"

And the moral of the story is . . .

Truth is not flexible or else it becomes something else.

Dad's Hat

One day Dad was roofing a house. It was hot to say the least. He had Clifford and myself helping him. I was on top of the house with Dad, and Clifford was bringing the shingles up to the top of the ladder for me to take to Dad. Finally when we had all the shingles on the roof, Clifford came up. We were laying out the shingles, and Dad was nailing them down. It was hot. Dad pulled off his hat, laid it down on the roof and said he was going down for a drink of water, leaving Clifford and me on the roof. Clifford decided the wind might blow Dad's hat off the roof so he took a large roof tack and nailed Dad's hat to the roof. Dad comes back on the roof, grabs his hat, and half the brim was town off. Needless to say, Dad was upset to no end. He looked at us and said, "Who nailed my hat to the roof?" Well, neither of us said a word. So Dad grabbed a shingle and folded it and whipped both of us there on the roof.

I learned something that day, and it is that correction and punishment are more effective at higher elevations.

And the moral of the story is . . .

Discipline should be done on the spot or else it later turns into, "You shouldn't have done that."

My mother never said, "Wait until your dad gets home." She held court then and there.

Where Is There?

Many times I have been asked, "What does a chaplain do?" Well, he or she may not know until they get "there." And where is "there"? Well, "there" could be aboard a cruise ship where my wife Janie and I served as chaplains after I retired.

One such "there" was just off Christmas Island in the Pacific Ocean. The captain paged me one morning. I responded to be told that a lady aboard the ship had died. I met with the husband and assisted him with several calls back home. I stayed with him the rest of the day. He told me he did not know anyone on the ship. I met him the next morning for breakfast. He talked until noon. That afternoon I helped him make more calls. I stayed with him. We ate every meal together until we got to Hawaii which took three days. We talked, read scripture and prayed.

In Hawaii his son was there to meet him. He hugged me and thanked me and left with his son to go back to the states.

The chaplain was "there."

On another cruise while eating dinner the first night, Janie and I met two lovely ladies. The next day the two ladies saw Janie in one of the shops. One of them said, "Oh, you are the chaplain's wife. Could we talk to you?" So they talked.

They told Janie that both of their husbands had recently died just weeks apart. One was killed by a car that jumped the curb and ran over him. The other husband died from a sudden heart attack. They told Janie they were both school teachers and taught at the same school. They had been friends for years, and the deaths of their husbands brought them closer together so they decided to come on the cruise.

For the next five days Janie and the two ladies would meet for coffee, and other times they would talk. And Janie listened. They would cry, and knowing Janie, she might have cried with them.

Janie was "there."

Grief is talked out, not kept inside. Janie helped them to realize that.

People bring so much "baggage" on board a cruise ship. Examples of that are the death of a loved one (the baggage of grief), divorce (the baggage of betrayal), unfulfilled dreams (the baggage of runaways, home problems, work load, children's situations, etc). The list of baggage goes on and on. A cruise ticket can't cure or lighten the load of the baggage very much.

And the moral of the story is . . .

Everyone needs a priest, someone they can talk to without being criticized, someone they can confess to without being condemned, someone who will be truthful and dependable.

The chaplain is "there" to lighten the weight of the baggage that people carry.

A Get-Up

Time means different things to different people. You take an expectant mother who, in spite of complications, is loving every minute of it. Feeling movement in her body reminds her that she is a partner with God to create a being.

Having been a prison chaplain, I realized that a person serving time (sentence) for a crime committed looks at time quite differently. He or she is miserable every day, feeling the agony of confinement and the pain of being dehumanized. It is sometimes called "hard time." They all want their time commuted. They want their time to be shortened.

One day I asked an inmate how much time he had left to serve. He said, "Twenty-nine days and a get-up." He had thirty days, but he didn't count the last day, just called it the day to get up and go!

I soon found that many of the inmates used that same expression. To them it was like shortening their time by one day.

And the moral of the story is . . .

Time cannot be manipulated. I woke up one morning and I was eighty-five years, not young but old. Let's face it, time rolls on regardless of who you are or where you are or what you might have done or how you count time.

Mom Was There

I had a speaking engagement in another city that would take me away from home overnight, and I wanted my wife Janie to go with me. This meant we would have to make arrangements for our son regarding where he would stay. He insisted on staying at home. It would be on a Friday night and we would be home by noon the next day. So we agreed for him to stay at home.

As we were preparing to leave, Janie was giving Paul some instructions like don't let anyone in the house, keep doors locked, etc. Paul spoke up and said, "Mom, I am sixteen years old." His mother replied, "Yes, I know, Paul; I was there."

And the moral of the story is . . .

A mother's position always gives her certain rights and authority. Amen?

Greatest Joy of Life

In 1963 while I was chaplain at the Shelby County Penal Farm, I was responsible for the blood donation program for St. Jude Children's Hospital. Each Saturday our prison bus would take those inmates who wished to donate blood to St. Jude. After the inmates had donated their blood, the hospital would feed them a good meal (much better than prison food) and give each of them five dollars.

One day I realized that the inmates had given over one thousand pints of blood. The question I asked myself was, "How can I thank the inmates that had donated and encourage others to give?" While talking to several inmates about my question, one of the inmates suggested that I invite Danny Thomas to come to the prison and thank them. Knowing that Danny did come to St. Jude from time to time, I decided to give it a try. I wrote Danny a letter and to my surprise, I got a response in a couple of weeks telling me that Danny would come to the prison on his next trip to St. Jude.

On the day that Danny was to come, the warden cancelled all work detail and other activities so that the entire prison population could hear Danny's presentation.

Danny started by telling stories and for thirty-five minutes had the inmates laughing. They just loved it. Danny had come to see them. Then he stopped the fun and talked about St. Jude, its service to the children and their families and the hospital's need and hope for the future. I shall never forget Danny's closing words. I have quoted them many times, "The greatest joy and fulfillment I get out of life is to be able to help people."

And the moral of the story is . . .

There is no greater joy than that of helping others.

Who Makes Your Day?

When I returned from the Navy, I worked as a bookkeeper at an automobile dealership. The parts manager at the dealership would occasionally go home for lunch. One day on his way home, Miss Sadie ran a stop sign and ran into Robert's car. It did quite a bit of damage. Robert jumped out of his car, looked at the damage and said, "Miss Sadie, I am so sorry; it was my fault." Miss Sadie said, "No, Robert, it was my fault." Robert said, "Oh, no, Miss Sadie, it was my fault!" Miss Sadie said, "Now, Robert, I taught you in the fifth grade and I know you are an honest person so why do you keep saying it was your fault?" Robert replied, "I knew you drove on Thursdays."

And the moral of the story is:

It is much better if you make your own day.

A Good Dream
That Came True

I was asked to be part of a program that would require fifty ministers, each one to be assigned to a different church in New Brunswick, Canada. I had to bring a person with music skills. I took the music minister of the church where I was interim pastor at the time. My assignment was a Baptist church on Campobello Island.

As I drove across the bridge at Lubec, Maine, over to the island, I thought about what the next seven days would be like. I must admit that I was not very encouraged.

The little island, nine miles long and three miles wide, was beautiful. The little town on the upper end of the island, Wilson Beach, had two stores, a post office and a church. The residents were mostly commercial fishermen. It also had a fish processing factory that had closed down two years before I arrived. On the lower end of the island were Roosevelt Park and the home where President Roosevelt and his family spent summers. There was one café on the island, about midway of the island, and another store, but no gas station or health clinic.

The second day I was there, one of the men of the church took me to a site about two miles from the church.

There he shared with me how the church had acquired an old ocean-front farm back in 1958 to be used as a youth/children's camp. The men and women of the church built three cottages and repaired some of the beautiful old farmhouse. The camp was opened and ran until about 1985 at which time the fishery plant closed, cutting off most of the financial support for the camp.

The camp had grown up in weeds, and repair was needed on the cottages and the house. The person showing me the site stressed how much the camp was needed and how the church felt about the need for the camp. I visited the campsite every day, dreaming of how I could help reopen the camp. I asked several of the men in the church if they thought we could reopen the camp. I received such a positive response I felt I had to do something. So that last night when I had finished my presentation, I asked those present to stay for a while. I told them my dream to reopen the camp. I let them talk. It was all positive. So I made a commitment to them that I would do all I could to help open the camp.

I came back home and told my story to the church where I was interim pastor. The next summer thirty-four men and women in that church went with me. We repaired, painted, cut weeds and grass, made a sign for the camp entrance, and did a number of other things. Members of the church would come to the camp each night and feed us. We would sing and pray and talk about what we could do to help the camp. The next summer the camp was opened, and I took my youngest son Paul with me. He stayed two months and served as the assistant to the camp director.

The camp is still operating. It has expanded its services. A college in St. John's uses it a week each year for a retreat for its executive board. Other churches use it from time to time. They now have a week for a mothers' retreat and other such groups.

I have tried to continue to help. The camp needed hymn books. I contacted a church where I had served as interim pastor, and the church sent one hundred hymnals. Through the years I have continued to try to help. Without even thinking of his giving support for the camp, I told the camp's story to a friend who sent the camp a check for five thousand dollars. Year after year for five years I sent helpers for the camp. I took music ministers for three years. They taught children and adult choirs.

I sent a group of five men (carpenters) to build a new kitchen and dining room. The church sold timber on the property and furnished the kitchen with the very best equipment.

And the moral of the story is . . .

One day thirteen hundred miles from home in another country I had a dream, and with a lot of help my dream came true. It was a good dream. When have you had a good dream?

My Gravy Recipe

When I was in college, I lived in one of the school's duplexes. Bob, my close friend, lived in the duplex next to me. As we were walking to our duplexes one day after we had just finished our final exams, Bob said, "Let's celebrate." So we went to the store and bought two pork chops and a can of biscuits.

While Bob was cooking the pork chops, he said, "I sure would love to have some good old gravy with these biscuits." I said, "That's no problem. I've seen my mother make gravy. I can make gravy." Bob said, "Okay, get ready to take over." I said, "Leave the grease in the skillet. I'll need it." Bob said, "What else do you need?" I said, "Flour." He said, "How much?" I said, "You have a scoop (it would hold about half a cup) there. Give me one scoop." Bob said, "Now we want plenty of gravy." I said, "Well, put another scoop in the skillet." Well, I mixed that flour with the grease and told Bob to bring me the milk. He brought me a quart of milk. I poured some in the skillet, and the gravy got real thick. I poured in more milk, and it continued to get thick! I kept pouring in the milk, and it got thicker and thicker until the skillet was full and I couldn't pour in any more milk. I just kept stirring, and lo and behold, it became a ball-looking thing. Bob said, "I believe we are going to have sliced gravy." Bob took a knife, sliced off a piece and put it in one of the biscuits.

And the moral of the story is . . .

Be careful about exposing your skills in public. Furthermore, good gravy recipes are not handed down through the genes. The same with character.

School Car Wash

When my oldest son got his driver's license and was just being allowed to take the car out alone, his school was having a car wash to raise money for the school band. He asked if he could take our car and go help at the car wash and also wash our car.

Now, our car was not just a car. It was the only car before or since that had been bought new. I had always bought used cars. It was a 1967 four-door with white sidewall tires. I took extra good care of it.

The morning went by fast. It was Saturday, and I had many things to do around the house. Finally I went inside the house and asked Janie when David was to come home. She said, "It is past time." I jumped in her car and went to the school. I knew that the car washing would be down on the football field. As I approached, I didn't see our car. I was shocked when I looked beyond the football field and saw an area that had no grass on it, nothing but Georgia red clay. Several boys and my son had wet the area, making it very slick. I watched as my car came barreling down (which means going fast) with David driving. When he got on the watered-down area, he hit the brakes. The car turned all the way around and stopped with David facing me.

And the moral of the story is . . .

Call my son if you ever need a precise definition of the word "grounded."

Just In Case

I have a friend who told me about an experience he had with his first-grade daughter.

The two of them were in the den one night after dinner. He was reading and she was writing. He said to her, "What are you writing?" She replied. "I am writing, 'Don't ring the bell,' twenty-five times." "Why are you writing the same thing twenty-five times?" he asked. She said, "Our teacher has a bell on her desk that she doesn't want anyone but herself to ring. Some of the kids have been ringing it, and she makes them write, 'Don't ring the bill,' twenty-five times." Her dad said, "Oh, you must have rung the bell." She replied, "No, I didn't ring the bell." He said, "Well, if you didn't ring the bell, why are you writing, 'Don't ring the bell,' twenty-five times?" She said, "Oh, that's just in case."

And the moral of the story is . . .

There is nothing like being prepared. Trust me.

The Cottage at Campobello

While going back and forth to Campobello to help with the youth/children's camp, I saw a small unoccupied cottage on the island overlooking Passamaquoddy Bay. It was a small two-story with a mansard roof. It was built in 1900, but no one had lived there since 1962. I knew it would need lots of work such as rewiring, new roof, new windows and doors, and a number of other things. So I inquired and was able to purchase it.

Many of the people in the little town of Wilson Beach were excited about the rebirth of the little cottage. When it was finished, I had an open house and invited all to come by. Many told of their memories of the old house. I had found old newspapers and other items in the attic and in the root cellar which was under the kitchen floor. I displayed all those for the visitors to see.

It was a good time for all. Also, it gave me another opportunity to share with them how important the camp would be in the lives of their children.

I chose not to tell or show them two other items I found in the root cellar. Those items included a beautiful little cup and two empty bottles. They were very well hidden. I had been there over a year before I just happened to find them. No doubt they had been there for many, many years.

The cup belonged to a lady. No man would drink out of a beautiful little cup like that one. I gave the bottles to a bottle collector who told me they would date back to around 1910-1920 and were used to bottle sherry.

And the moral of the story is . . .

Don't show and tell everything you know. It is not necessary.

Nickname

My dad had a nickname. It was "Burnt." His cousin Marvin gave him that name after an experience my dad had one night.

The old house we lived in was extra cold in the winter. All we had was a fireplace and the kitchen stove. At night my mother would heat her irons that she ironed our clothes with and put them in the bed to keep our feet warm. We all wore flannel gowns that my mother made on her sewing machine.

Well, one night Dad had us all in the bed and he put on his flannel gown and backed up to the fire to warm before he hopped into bed. He got too close to the fire and it caught his gown on fire!

It burned his backside to the extent that he had to stand up to eat for four days. From that time on, his cousin called him "Burnt."

And the moral of the story is . . .

Fire is no respecter of persons. If you get too close, it will burn you.

Our Children's Taste Vs. Ours

Our oldest son David was never idle. He enjoyed the outdoors, but most of all he seemed to enjoy making or repairing things. He built model cars and airplanes. He also loved to repair toys, getting them back in working order.

After finishing high school, he chose not to go to college. He went to work for the Internal Revenue Service. (He recently retired from the IRS after more than thirty-six years in the computer department.)

After he had worked there for a few months, he wanted to move away from home. That was okay. He worked hard and managed his money well.

He rented a small apartment. It had a living room area, bedroom, small kitchen, and bathroom. It was small but just what he needed.

After he had been in his apartment a few days, Janie and I decided to take him a few things for his apartment. Janie bought throw rugs, towels, a broom, and other things. She chose the colors of the throw rugs and towels she thought he would like. She wanted his first apartment to look neat and attractive.

When we knocked, David opened the door and invited us in. And what was the first thing we saw? There was a Volkswagen motor on the floor right in the middle of the small living room!

And the moral of the story is . . .

The taste of our children can be quite different from ours. (Their taste may change when they marry and have children of their own.)

Aisle Seat # 26C

While serving on the staff of the Home Mission Board, I would fly Early Bird and Owly Bird flights so I could be at home with my family and save on my expenses as well.

One morning I flew an Early Bird to St. Louis. I rushed that morning and asked myself several times, "Now why am I doing this, getting up at 4:30 to get ready and drive twenty miles to the airport?"

Well, I made my 6:30 flight and was seated in an aisle seat. I greeted a couple who occupied the other two seats. The plane was still loading. It seemed we would be late getting off the ground. I said to the couple I had just greeted, "It seems that we are running a little late." The husband spoke up and said, "Yes, and I think we are partly to blame." I asked, "Why would you say that?" He said, "We flew into Atlanta from Florida, and they had to transfer the casket containing our seventeen-year-old daughter to this plane."

After I expressed my condolences and told them that I was a chaplain, I asked what had happened to bring about her death. They told me that, along with several other matters, she had problems adjusting after finishing high school. The husband said, "She just went down to the beach a few nights ago and shot herself in the head with one of my antique pistols."

Then they told me they were taking her body back to St. Louis for burial. I let them talk all the way to St. Louis. We had a brief prayer as the plane landed. They wanted my address, and for several years I received Christmas cards from them.

And the moral of the story is . . .

I didn't have to ask myself why I was assigned to seat #26C that early morning. Those things don't just happen. There is a higher power who can assign seats.

Ironed Blue Jeans

One morning Janie was ironing a pair of blue jeans for our youngest son Paul to wear to school. Suddenly she heard a scream coming from Paul saying, "Mom, don't iron the jeans." Janie thought she was doing him a little extra favor to make him look nice. Then he said, "Mom, if you iron those jeans, I will be the only Tucker High School student with a crease in his jeans!"

And the moral of the story is . . .

Sometimes it is okay to look like the rest of them.

A Child's Uniqueness

During my college days, I pastored a small country church in West Tennessee. Several years prior to my coming, two people had died of causes I do not know. One was a young married lady, and the other was a young married man. As I mentioned, several years had passed and the two living spouses began to date, eventually asking me if I would marry them. The young lady had a five-year-old son, a very cute and sharp fellow.

The day of the wedding, the church was packed with people. It was one of the first weddings of my ministry. The five-year-old son of the bride was allowed to sit on the front pew just in front of the bride's mother. The little fellow was excited, moving around continuously and smiling. When his mother was coming down the aisle, he stood up like everyone else and pretended to walk toward her. She shook her head, and he went back and sat down. Things went fine until I said to the husband, "You may now kiss the bride." While the kiss was taking place, the little five-year-old stood up and loudly exclaimed, "They have been doing a lot of that lately."

Well, I had never heard that much laughter in a church, I assure you. I usually have a closing prayer after the kiss, but I said to the bride and groom, "No prayer; go," and they marched down the aisle. Yes, the little fellow followed down the aisle right behind them!

And the moral of the story is . . .

A child will tell and show you like it is.

Known By Hair Style

My brother Clifford and I walked into Mr. Chamber's store one day to buy some thread Mama had sent us to get. A man walked in the store who was a stranger to both of us. He looked down at us and said, "You are Elton Hart's boys, aren't you?" Clifford said, "Yes, but how did you know that?" The man said, "I could tell when I saw your haircut."

You see, Dad cut our hair by placing a bowl on our heads and cutting all the hair below the bowl. And he did it with hand clippers, not electric clippers. He had to squeeze the handles together, causing gaping results.

It was a happy day when I could go to the barbershop and get a "store bought" hair cut.

And the moral of the story is . . .

Leave it to Dad. He will fix it or break it trying.

So What

After worship services one Sunday morning, a couple invited me to go to their home for lunch. I gladly accepted.

While we were eating, the wife asked me if I would have another serving of the casserole. I said, "Yes." While she was serving it, the husband said, "You know, preacher, if a doctor can't tell you what's wrong with you, he calls it a virus. If a woman can't tell what she has cooked, she calls it a casserole."

And the moral of the story is . . .

So what? You don't have to know everything to get the job done.

Life Is Hard Sometimes

While a student at the seminary, I pastored the Lystra Baptist Church. Another student pastored a church six miles away.

In the church where I pastored, there was a young lady who married a young man who had been a member of the church just six miles away. At the time they were both members of the church where I pastored.

One Sunday morning, the young man's father attended the church where I pastored. After we shared greetings, he informed me that he was a pilot. That afternoon his son and the young lady's father and brother were flying with him to Nag's Head to see what damage might have happened to his cabin as a result of the storm that past week.

That afternoon as the plane took off, it clipped the top of the trees, causing the plane to crash.

It caught on fire and burned all four of the men to death.

That afternoon the young lady, who was soon to birth a boy, lost her father, her father-in-law, her brother and her husband.

And the moral of the story is . . .

Life is hard and we cannot be prepared for all of its hurts, but with help we can survive.

Hand-Me-Downs

One of the favorite times for us back home was when our cousin Junior came to see us. He was one year older than my oldest brother. We lived out in the country, and he lived in the big city of Memphis. In the summer he would come and stay a week or so with us, and on many occasions his parents would bring him to see us on Sunday afternoons.

Junior's mother was a very thoughtful person. From time to time she would bring clothes that he had outgrown and give them to my older brother. Then my brother would wear them until he outgrew them, and he would give them to me. Well, I'll just tell you that when clothes have been worn by two growing rough-and-tough boys, the third receiver never looks too sharp.

But one day I heard my mother tell my dad that I needed a new sweater. I really got excited! Dad took me to town and bought me a sweater. It was one of those with a huge roll-down collar. You talk about walking tall, I was walking tall! My own store-bought sweater. No hand-me-down. Bought for me!

And the moral of the story is . . .

Very few things can compare with your own ownership of something. Discovering a talent, receiving an earned title or degree, ownership of a home, your own little baby, and the list goes on. Bought just for me.

My Dad's Work Ethic

I grew up on a little farm in the southwest part of Tennessee. My dad was a sharecropper until I was thirteen years of age. Then with World War II and the demand for carpenters, Dad stopped farming and became a carpenter. Farming had been a struggle through the years, seeming never to get us out of debt. Mom and Dad had worked so hard trying to keep five children clothed, fed, and in school.

About a year after Dad started doing carpenter work, he bought five acres of land and built us a house. We had electric light for the first time! One light hanging from the ceiling in each room. I can remember Dad tying a string on one of the lights so we kids could reach it and turn on the light!

Dad did good work, and he was never without work. He worked hard. His specialty was built-in kitchen cabinets. (This was before cabinets were made in factories like they are today.) Dad had a waiting list. I was his helper when I was not in school.

I never shall forget the day he had finished building a set of cabinets. As we were gathering up the tools to leave, he stood back, just looked at the finished job for a while, and then he said, "Not a bad job if I do have to say so myself."

And the moral of the story is . . .

I learned my work ethic from watching my dad, just like it is supposed to be.

Choosing the Right Paint

While I was Director of Chaplaincy for the Tennessee Department of Corrections, one of my tasks was to place a staff chaplain at the main prison. The prison had never had a fulltime chaplain. Both the staff and inmates were looking forward to his coming.

The warden authorized an office space inside the walls for the new chaplain. The space needed painting and some repairing which several inmates were assigned to do. When they had finished the repair, they asked a staff member the whereabouts of the paint. The staff member made a joke out of their question and replied, "I guess you will have to steal it."

Now, the prison had a paint factory where paint was made for road signs and license plates.

At that time the prison had several factories inside the wall of the prison. There was a clothing factory where the inmates made the clothing for all the inmates, and a license plate factory where the inmates made all the license plates for the state of Tennessee. Also they had the paint factory where they made all the paint used to paint state buildings, road signs, etc. So the inmates took it upon themselves to steal (they called it borrowing) a couple of gallons of paint down at the paint factory!

The day the inmates finished the painting of the office, I had not gone by to see it. But I got a call that night about 10:15 pm from the captain of the guard. He told me that when he turned on the flood lights to make the 10:00 o'clock check, the lights were on in the newly painted chaplain's office. He said that he sent two security guards to check it out. They came back laughing and one said, "The lights were not on; the inmates have painted the office with luminous paint." The luminous paint was the type used to paint the road signs and center lines in the roads so they would glow in the dark. So when the flood lights were turned on, the new chaplain's office glowed!

And the moral of the story is . . .

You can be sure your "borrowing" will find you out.

London Eye

While in London, my wife and I rode the London Eye. What an experience! Our thoughts were that it would be like the Ferris wheel and go round and round. But we found out differently. It makes only one round! The idea is not to ride, but to see. The one rotation lasted about twenty-five minutes. Each compartment could accommodate about twenty people. There were seats in the center, yet there was plenty of room to walk around.

What a thrill to see London in that fashion. My wife and I did not sit down. We just walked around the whole twenty-five minutes and spotted the various points of interest. What an experience! I wanted our grandchildren and others to experience the same.

And the moral of the story is . . .

When you reach the point of wishing others could experience the same as you have, you have reached a higher level of appreciation for those who made such experiences possible.

Stand Up Straight

While we were in Pisa, Italy, my wife took a picture of the Leaning Tower. But when we got home and had the picture developed, we had a good laugh! The Leaning Tower was perfectly upright. It was not leaning at all! But all the other buildings, trees, and flowers were leaning.

And the moral of the story is . . .

There is more to photography than light and being in focus.

Blessed Are the Flexible

A dear friend of mine, who was a minister of church music, went with me to Canada to participate in a simultaneous religious program involving fifty churches in New Brunswick. Like myself, he had never been to Canada. All we knew was that we were to go to a small church on Campobello Island.

My friend's questions were, "How do I prepare for this event and what do I take with me?" Then my friend and I began to ask other questions. "Will they accept us?" "Will the people even come to the services led by strangers?" With all of our questions and with a little fear and trembling, we arrived at the church. We were met by a couple that in a short time had answered all our questions and had us feeling as if Billy Graham and Bev Shea had come to the island.

The church had no pastor at the time so we had to manage the best we could. My friend announced there would be choir rehearsal before the worship each night. Then he put together a children's choir and taught them songs. By the middle of the week the adult choir was full. Also, by the middle of the week most of those attending the worship services came early so they could experience the choir rehearsal.

It was a great week. By the end of the week people were standing around the walls and in the vestibule because there were no seats left.

But don't think everything worked out perfectly. No, no. But to walk into a situation in another country prepared with very few if any guidelines of any type, the event turned out to be an experience both of us cherish to this day.

As we drove across the bridge going off the island heading home, I asked my friend, "How did things work out as well as they did?"

And the moral of the story is . . .

His answer, "Blessed are the flexible for they shall not be bent out of shape."

VW Vs. Tree

In the office where I worked, the staff was almost like family. From time to time we would share things that had given us concern or distress. For example, one Monday morning four of us were in the break room talking. When two other staff members walked in, we asked how things were going with them. One said, "Better than we were on Saturday." We asked what had happened on Saturday and were given the details. One of the fellows had a tree in his yard that needed to come down. The two of them decided they would tackle the job. After looking the situation over, they came up with the idea that they could tie a chain to the tree and then tie the other end of the chain to the back bumper of their VW. With a slight pull of the VW, the tree should fall in the direction they wanted. One fellow got in the VW and the other one started cutting the tree with his chainsaw. When the tree was about to fall, the fellow with the chainsaw signaled to the other one to give the chain a pull. Well, the tree fell where it wanted to, dragging the VW across the yard to end up in the limbs of the tree with only its two front wheels touching the ground.

And the moral of the story is . . .

Nothing hurts like a shoe that doesn't fit, VW vs. tree.

Sometimes we are just left hanging in spite of all our planning.

Nothing

My wife and I had been aboard a ship for a number of days, long enough that my wife said, "I am not having a dessert tonight; I've eaten enough sweets." Well, the waiter who had served us each night and was such a nice and jolly person asked us, "What would you prefer for dessert?" My wife said, "Nothing." Soon he brought her a plate that had written on it "nothing" in chocolate syrup.

And the moral of the story is:

That's the way it is with life. The only thing you get for nothing is nothing.

Request of Three Little Girls

My office was in downtown Atlanta about twenty miles away. To deal with the heavy Atlanta traffic, I would go to work early in the morning and return home about mid-afternoon. There were three little girls (ages five to seven) who lived a couple of doors down the street from our home.

Almost every afternoon when I pulled in my driveway, the three little girls would run up to the car as I was getting out. They would ask me to pull them in their wagon or play soccer with my oldest son's soccer ball. Sometimes they would ask me questions. That gave me an opportunity to ask them trick questions, such as, "What goes up and never comes down?" (Your age.) I enjoyed the girls' company as much as they enjoyed mine.

One day I came home early. The girls were not there to meet me. I got out of my car and went in the house. About thirty minutes later, there was a knock at the door. My wife went to the door, and there were the three little girls. One of them asked my wife, "Can your husband come out and play?"

And the moral of the story is . . .

The request of a child can be stronger than the demands of an adult.

We Can't Fix Everything

One night I was traveling on a train from Hamburg to Berchtesgaden in Germany. At one of the stops, two boys boarded the train and sat across the aisle from me. The oldest one looked to be about ten years old and the smallest one about six. The oldest boy had a paper bag that appeared to have clothing in it. Both boys were extremely dirty, their clothing as well as their hands and faces. The exception was the youngest boy's thumb on his right hand. It was clean and white. I questioned myself why that thumb was so clean and white until I saw him put that thumb in his mouth and suck it.

I wanted to help them in some way. I couldn't speak their language, and I was a total stranger from another country. So I just sat there looking at two dirty little boys all alone on a train at night. Where were they going, and where were their parents? "What will happen to them?" I asked myself. Feeling as helpless as I could possibly feel, I wanted to help them.

I recall another time when I had the same helpless feeling. My wife and I were on our way to the airport in Mumbai, India, at 1:30 in the morning. When the taxi stopped for a red light, people crowded around the taxi. The driver made it very clear that we were to keep our doors locked and our windows up. Ten or more people were pecking on our windows. They wanted money. They looked hungry. They were desperate. Some of them had children in their arms. We looked out our windows and saw hundreds of people sleeping on the ground or just walking or standing around. The light changed and slowly the people surrounding us moved away so the taxi could continue.

My wife and I wanted to help, but we couldn't. We were helpless. We couldn't do a thing.

And the moral of the story is . . .

There are some things we simply cannot fix, no matter how much we might desire to.

Crying Is a Gift

There is a church in Macon, Georgia, that has a sign on the campus that reads "Crying Room" with an arrow pointing to a particular door. The sign shows directions to the nursery for those who have babies.

At first I didn't know what the sign was talking about. I thought maybe that church was saying it allowed crying. I know some churches that don't allow crying! I suppose they might have a sign pointing to the sanctuary entrance that reads "No Crying Allowed." As if we adults don't need to cry.

One day when I was about sixteen years old, I walked into my mother's bedroom and found her seated on the side of the bed crying. I said, "Mama, why are you crying? What's the matter? I don't want you to cry." She then told me why she was crying. It was Clifford, my oldest brother. He was off in the war. She had not heard from him in over a month. He was her first son and had been sickly as a child. Without her consent, he joined the Navy. The last letter she received from him told her that he was in the Palau Islands in the Pacific Ocean.

She couldn't hold it back; she had to find a place to cry. Then I got to crying with her. After a while we stood up and had a prayer for Clifford and dried our tears.

I didn't try to stop Mama from crying. She needed to cry, and so did I.

And the moral of the story is . . .

Crying is another one of God's gifts. It is like kissing the skinned knee of a child. It makes the hurt feel better. A good cry is God's kiss that makes us feel better.

My Name

At birth I was given the name Alfred Carl Hart. I was named after my great uncle, Alfred Samuel Atkinson, who was a brother to my paternal grandmother. I was called Alfred until I was about five years old. From that time until this day, I have been called Carl.

My great-grandmother died, leaving three acres and an old house. Now my grandmother thought she should get the three acres and old house because she had taken care of her mother for eight years before her death. There was no will so her brother, Uncle Alfred, rushed off to the courthouse and acquired a quick claim deed to the property.

From that day on Grandmother and Uncle Alfred never spoke to one another again. My grandmother refused to even speak his name before her death thirty-four years later.

Thus, Grandmother started calling me by my middle name of Carl so she would not have to say her brother's name. Being the strong person that she was, she insisted that everyone else call me Carl. So that is why I am called by my middle name.

And the moral of the story is . . .

Hate is such a cruel thing. It can destroy a family's love for one another for years. The Apostle Paul said, "Do not let the sun go down on your anger."

God Will Have the Final Word

Two of the most moving experiences of my life happened in different parts of the world. The first was in Germany. I visited one of the camps where Hitler housed the Jews and slaughtered them by the thousands. From there I went to Berchtesgaden in south Germany and visited the underground bunkers where Hitler could hide if need be. Nearby was Hitler's personal retreat lodge which I visited as well. It was on a high peak overlooking the mountains. I browsed through the lodge and then went out on the veranda overlooking the mountains. Standing there I experienced one of the emptiest feelings I had ever felt. It was mixed feelings as well, ones of grief, anger, and shame. It is very difficult to put in words my feelings. Then I wondered how one man could do all that Hitler did. Ego plus hate is a very dangerous monster. I asked myself if there could ever be another such monster with such power and hate.

My second experience was in India in one of the homes of Gandhi who was Prime Minister of India (1966-77, 1980-84). I had read about Gandhi and had even seen a movie revealing his leadership. He led people rather than demanding them. He gave them something to live for instead of taking away their lives. He knew truth and practiced it. He loved people and expressed it.

Standing there in Gandhi's home that day I had a flashback of my trip to Hitler's retreat lodge. I thought of the difference in the two men. I had deep positive feelings for one and negative feelings for the other.

Then I had a feeling that gave me hope and assurance.

And the moral of the story is . . .

Let us never forget that God will have the final word, not man or country or weapons or thinkers.

Printed in the United States
By Bookmasters